N

D

Daniel P. Horan, OFM

LITURGICAL PRESS

Collegeville, Minnesota

litpress.org

Nihil Obstat: Rev. Robert C. Harren, J.C.L., *Censor Librorum*

Imprimatur: ✠ Most Rev. Patrick M. Neary, C.S.C., Bishop of St. Cloud, July 22, 2024

Cover design by Monica Bokinskie. Cover art courtesy of Getty Images.

ISSN: 1552-8782; 2692-6407 (e-book)

ISBN: 978-0-8146-6799-6   978-0-8146-6801-6 (ebook)

Introduction

In 1958, Thomas Merton wrote a short essay titled "Ash Wednesday." In it he makes an important point, one worth meditating on as we begin our Lenten journey: "Even the darkest moments of the liturgy are filled with joy, and Ash Wednesday, the beginning of the Lenten fast, is a day of happiness, a Christian feast. It cannot be otherwise, as it forms part of the great Easter cycle."

What I love about Merton's introduction to the Lenten season is the admonition that we ought not succumb to the mistaken belief that Lent is solely a time for doom and gloom, mourning and lament, as important as those feelings are. Instead, we are to remember that Lent only has meaning in light of Easter—that the season of penance, prayer, and discernment into which we enter is a preparation for the celebration of the Paschal Mystery that we are already a part of now. It's an opportunity to reflect on what is distinctive about our faith, where we might grow, where God might be challenging us, and how to accept the divine invitation to enter into deeper relationships with one another, God, and all of creation.

Merton goes on to explain: "The Paschal Mystery is above all the mystery of life, in which the Church, by celebrating the death and resurrection of Christ, enters into the Kingdom of Life which He has established once for all by His definitive victory over sin and death. . . . Lent then is not a season of punishment so much as one of healing." It is in this spirit that

Merton anticipates the wisdom of Pope Francis who, in his apostolic exhortation *Evangelii Gaudium*, writes: "There are Christians whose lives seem like Lent without Easter. . . . Joy adapts and changes, but it always endures, even as a flicker of light born of our personal certainty that, when everything is said and done, we are infinitely loved."

The reflections that follow in this little book are invitations to remember that Lent is always tied to the joy of Easter, to the Christian hope expressed in the resurrection. The way we come to know that joy and hope, even amid the suffering and struggles of our world, is by becoming people of Scripture and prayer. Consider these reflections an invitation to deeper engagement with Scripture this Lent. And may the meditations and prayers that accompany them provide you with food for your own spiritual journey.

Daniel P. Horan, OFM

Reflections

What's on the Inside Counts

Readings: Joel 2:12-18; 2 Cor 5:20–6:2; Matt 6:1-6, 16-18

Scripture:
Rend your hearts, not your garments,
 and return to the LORD, your God. (Joel 2:13)

Reflection: It has always amused me that in today's Gospel,
Jesus goes to great lengths to teach his followers "not to
perform righteous deeds in order that people may see them,"
and then, within minutes of hearing this proclamation, we
line up to receive a big smudge of ashes on our foreheads
for the whole world to see!

As funny as our liturgical practice of receiving ashes after
this Gospel may seem, we shouldn't overlook an important
lesson that threads today's readings together regarding what
God expects of us. God is inviting us to explore what *motivates*
our spiritual practices. *Why* do we do what we do during
Lent? To be seen by others? To prove something to ourselves
or God? To show off within our faith community or demon-
strate our religious "chops"? None of these motivations reflect what God is asking of us. But, if we are honest, they are
often the source of our penitential practices.

The prophet Joel cuts right to the heart of the matter when
he announces: "Rend your hearts, not your garments, / and
return to the LORD, your God." It is what is inside that really

matters. God doesn't care about superficial gestures or performances, nor is God interested in what others think about us or whether they are impressed by what we do externally. God calls us to be transformed internally, to return to God with our hearts and minds.

Meditation: It can be easy to get caught up in the external practices typically associated with the Lenten season. Do I spend more time worrying about what to "give up" or what to "take on" than I do about my relationships with God, others, and the entirety of creation? What does it mean for me to "return to the Lord" this Lent?

Prayer: God of mercy, you know me better than I know myself. Help me embrace your love, and change my desire for external affirmation into a desire for internal transformation. Help me return to you this Lent.

What It Means to Be Alive

Readings: Deut 30:15-20; Luke 9:22-25

Scripture:
"What profit is there for one to gain the whole world yet lose or forfeit himself?" (Luke 9:25)

Reflection: What does it mean to truly live? Sure, one can breathe and have a heartbeat, but is that enough? As God's prophet, Moses conveys to the people an image of what it means not just to live but to *be alive*. Right relationship with God, just relationships with neighbors, following the way of the Lord—this is how one finds true life and prosperity.

But too often we don't trust the word of the prophets, we don't walk in God's ways, nor do we keep God's "commandments, statutes and decrees" (Deut 30:16). Instead, we convince ourselves that freedom is really about doing whatever we want, whenever we want, regardless of how it affects us or others. Yet, as the late Jesuit theologian Karl Rahner famously said, our dependence on God and our authentic freedom are not opposed to one another. Rather, the more we embrace our reliance on God, follow God's will, and obey God's commands, the freer we actually are. To most people, this may seem at best counterintuitive and at worst simply absurd.

Jesus also preaches a word of counterintuitive wisdom in today's Gospel when he talks about desiring to lose one's life in order to save it. But what *kind* of life are we talking about? Jesus, like Moses before him, warns that if we are clinging to life in that narrow sense of freedom ("I can do whatever I want"), that is really no life at all. We must lose that way of being and instead embrace the true freedom that comes with doing God's will, freedom that will require taking up our crosses and following Christ.

Meditation: What is my sense of freedom? Who sets the itinerary of my life journey? Do I choose merely to live and get by, or do I seek to be fully alive in God's Spirit?

Prayer: God of pilgrimage, guide me on the path you have laid out before me. Strengthen my heart and will to love you, walk in your ways, and keep your commandments. Do not allow me to be led astray.

Real Sacrifice

Readings: Isa 58:1-9a; Matt 9:14-15

Scripture:
Do not fast as you do today
  to make your voice heard on high! (Isa 58:4; NABRE)

Reflection: Does God really want us to eat less chocolate or have fewer alcoholic drinks this Lent? As silly as this question may seem, it arises from a genuine concern that goes back at least to the time of the prophet Isaiah, as we see in today's first reading.

What is it that God really asks us to do when we fast? For many contemporary Christians, this question is answered by some form of voluntary deprivation of something one enjoys: "I'm giving this up for Lent." But if you scratch the surface of this well-intentioned practice, it doesn't take long to reveal the potential emptiness of such an act. Scripture is clear that this sort of fast is not what God cares about most.

Isaiah reminds his hearers (and us) that fasting is not simply about foregoing the excesses of our choosing, but a call to embrace transformative practices that bring our attitudes and actions closer to God's will. Isaiah explains that God doesn't want the fasting half-measures already in practice. God wants us to exercise real justice by freeing the wrongly imprisoned, lifting the burdened out of misery, sharing our resources with others, giving shelter to the homeless, and otherwise not abandoning those at the margins of our societies.

If abstaining from some material pleasures like dessert or drink reminds you to fast in this more embodied, practical, and demanding way, then good. If not, then perhaps today's readings are an invitation to forego this practice. The Gospel reminds us, after all, that Jesus and his followers did not "fast" in the way others did in his time. What matters most is how we live and treat others. What we need to "give up" this Lent is our old way of being.

Meditation: What is God calling me to do this Lent? What practices of generosity, love, and justice can I focus on in my attitudes and actions? Where do I need to grow in love of God and neighbor?

Prayer: God of justice, you call us to "rend our hearts, not our garments." Change my heart to look toward and not away from those in need. Help me see where injustice exists around me, and give me the strength to call it out, respond in love, and care for those before me.

Sinners Called by God

Readings: Isa 58:9b-14; Luke 5:27-32

Scripture:
"I have not come to call the righteous to repentance but sinners." (Luke 5:32)

Reflection: Today's first reading picks up where yesterday's left off. But a few chapters earlier in Isaiah, God relayed to the people a message that summarizes the Lenten readings before us: "For as the heavens are higher than the earth, / so are my ways higher than your ways, / my thoughts higher than your thoughts" (Isa 55:9).

It is striking how God's ways are often vastly different from our own. There is a certain simplicity in God's vision for the world: justice, peace, right relationships, inclusion, acceptance, forgiveness, and love. While most of us would say that we also want these things, our behavior frequently suggests otherwise. We are all sinners. This is partly why Isaiah spends so much time reminding his hearers of the need to be more like God and less like our often-selfish selves.

The universality of sinfulness is also what informs Jesus' rebuke to those who judge and dismiss his chosen company. To say that Jesus seeks sinners and not the righteous is to say that Jesus seeks all of us. We are all invited to reflect on the ways Jesus draws near, invites us to follow him, and calls us to be more Godlike in our thoughts and actions. What the Pharisees and scribes missed in Jesus' response was that he was also calling *them* to return to God and, as today's psalm encourages, to learn from God how to walk in the way of the Lord.

Meditation: In each season of life, we may find ourselves struggling with different temptations and actions that break the relationships we have with ourselves, others, and God. What is the sin that challenges me most today? How might "my ways" be more aligned with "God's ways" this Lent? Where am I struggling to follow Jesus or to accept that Jesus is calling *everyone*, even those I might dismiss or reject?

Prayer: God of mercy, your love is perfect, and your ways are so far above my ways. Help me examine my heart and conscience to see how I can better love, forgive, include, and work for justice. Strengthen my desire to follow you, and guide me in the way of your path.

It Is Written

Readings: Deut 26:4-10; Rom 10:8-13; Luke 4:1-13

Scripture:
The word is near you,
   in your mouth and in your heart. (Rom 10:8)

Reflection: Where do we turn to find answers or solutions when we're facing challenges and temptations? Today's reading from Paul's letter to the Romans gives us a helpful clue, especially when we read or hear it alongside today's Gospel.

While many people focus on the spectacular imagery of Jesus fasting in the desert, facing his metaphorical demons (and at least one literal demon), over the years I have found myself less interested in the temptations themselves and more attentive to Jesus' responses.

It is striking how unoriginal Jesus is in his responses to the tempter! While Jesus is remembered for his creative and sometimes surprising actions, parables, and preaching, in this case Jesus returns time and again to Sacred Scripture. Rather than coming up with any number of original responses, Jesus chooses to turn to the written word of God. In doing so, Jesus points us toward Scripture as the source of our response to temptation, too.

Paul reiterates this theme, calling our attention to the closeness of God's word and reminding us that the source of guidance we are looking for in the face of temptation is found in divine revelation. Everything we need to know about how God is calling us to live is laid out in Scripture—not in some literal interpretation or instruction book, but in the narrative that is God's story, which we proclaim in word and deed. If we become people of Scripture, imbued with this divine narrative of God's love for us and all creation, then we will have sure footing in handling the difficulties that confront us on the pilgrimage of life and faith.

Meditation: Sacred Scripture is important for Jesus' response to temptation. What role does the Bible play in my own life? How can Scripture play a more prominent role in my life and in my prayer?

Prayer: Word of God, you reveal the fullness of divine love to us in your life, death, and resurrection. You show us the way to respond to our questions and temptations. Help me to always keep your word close, so it may be always in my mouth and in my heart.

Owning Up and Asking Forgiveness

Readings: Lev 19:1-2, 11-18; Matt 25:31-46

Scripture:
"He will place the sheep on his right and the goats on his left." (Matt 25:33)

Reflection: Over the years, I have heard from Christians who find the story Jesus tells in today's Gospel terrifying. They assume Jesus is warning his followers of an impending judgment that is arbitrary or even capricious. After all, the sheep and the goats don't know that they are in either camp at the outset. "What if I messed up?" they wonder. "What if I'm a goat, and Jesus condemns me to hell?" Anxiety and fear rise at the thought of the end-time judgment.

But it's important to remember that both the would-be sheep and goats have the same information and are offered the same details. The message of Jesus is clear: when you love, serve, and care for your neighbor, you are loving, serving, and caring for God. Some people look back over their lives and realize they have been fulfilling God's will all along, even if they hadn't been doing so consciously. These sheep are affirmed.

Others are shown the ways they haven't done God's will. And what happens (or doesn't happen) next is important. Those who are labeled "goats" never acknowledge their wrongdoing, never take responsibility, and never ask for-giveness for their sins. Having been caught by surprise—just like the sheep—they have an opportunity to say: "I didn't realize! Lord, forgive me!" If they had responded this way, what do you think Jesus' response would be? Perhaps there would be no goats, just repentant sheep.

Meditation: Jesus never withholds love or forgiveness, but we can easily refuse both. For some people, this is because they feel undeserving of God's mercy, while for others such attitudes may be grounded in self-centeredness or arrogance. No one is condemned to become a "goat" without the op-portunity for repentance and reconciliation. The question is: Are we willing to recognize our need for God's love and mercy, and will we accept it?

Prayer: Lord, you know me completely. Help me know my-self better during this season of Lenten penance. Grant me the humility to recognize and own up to my failures to love so I can work toward reconciliation with others and you.

What Is Prayer?

Readings: Isa 55:10-11; Matt 6:7-15

Scripture:
"This is how you are to pray . . ." (Matt 6:9)

Reflection: There are many ways to pray. I recall learning this for the first time at my parish elementary school when my religion teacher introduced us to the acronym "ACTS," which stood for: *adoration, contrition, thanksgiving,* and *supplication*. Sure, as a fifth grader I wasn't yet familiar with most of those words, but something about this framework for prayer left a strong impression on me.

While there is nothing inherently wrong with thinking of prayer according to the ACTS acronym, I have come to realize some of its limitations. The biggest limitation is the implication that prayer is something that is primarily initiated by us and that it is largely a speaking or thinking activity.

In today's Gospel we get a very different sense of prayer. At first it seems that Jesus is merely giving his followers a formula, words to recite again and again. And, truthfully, many of us approach the Our Father in that way. But within the language of the Our Father itself, we are told what prayer truly is. Prayer is about *doing* God's will so that the kingdom of God can come into existence. We will know this is accomplished because earth will look like heaven.

Coincidentally, the very word "ACTS" suggests something of the same reality: prayer is what we communicate to God by our way of being in the world, not just in our words but also in our deeds.

Meditation: After Jesus instructs his followers on how to pray, he says: "If you forgive others their transgressions, your heavenly Father will forgive you" (Matt 6:14; NABRE). Forgiveness, mercy, charity—this is how we are called to act in the world. If we truly want to pray as Jesus taught us, we will forgive others as Jesus did and love one another as Jesus first loved us.

Prayer: God of all people, you call us to right relationship with one another and all of creation. For the times when I have harmed others, withheld love, or refused to forgive those who have harmed me, grant me your mercy. Give me the grace to do your will so I may participate in the arrival of your kingdom and contribute to making this earth as it is in heaven.

Challenging Our Expectations

Readings: Jonah 3:1-10; Luke 11:29-32

Scripture:
"Set out for the great city of Nineveh, and announce to it the message that I will tell you." (Jonah 3:2)

Reflection: Despite the widespread fascination with the large fish in the book of Jonah, the story is less about that odd scene (Jonah's failed escape plan to avoid God's call) and more about expectations. I have always believed that Jonah is the most honest of the would-be prophets in the Old Testament. All of them receive a call from God, and all of them attempt to escape it. Moses attempts five avoidance strategies, Jeremiah complains that he's too young, and Amos claims he must tend to his farm and family. But it is Jonah who literally walks away from God and the city he has been called to serve—that is, until God catches up with him!

Jonah views the people of Nineveh as his enemies, which results in two expectations. First, Jonah believes the Ninevites are undeserving of God's call to conversion and salvation. Second, even if Jonah is willing to preach God's message to them, he doesn't believe they will listen. In fact, Jonah seems confident that the Ninevites will harm him in some way. He has very low expectations.

This is where the story gets interesting, and Jonah's expectations are flipped entirely upside down. Not only do the people of Nineveh heed his prophetic word, but they do so in record time. The Bible tells us he's not even a third of the way through the city when everyone starts embracing practices of penance, including the king! Jonah is left to confront the gap between his expectations and God's.

Let's allow Jonah's story to have the same effect on us as we examine our own assumptions and expectations this Lent.

Meditation: So often we can be like Jonah, dead set on our own views, judgments, prejudices, and expectations of others. Are there individuals or groups of people that I dismiss as unworthy of outreach or even God's love? When God calls me to the peripheries or to unfamiliar places, do I run away like Jonah?

Prayer: God of mercy, the call of Jonah reminds us of our baptismal call to be missionary disciples to all in this world. Help me open my heart and mind to those I may be inclined to dismiss, ignore, or even despise. Show me the way.

Living the Golden Rule

Readings: Esth C:12, 14-16, 23-25; Matt 7:7-12

Scripture:
"Do to others whatever you would have them do to you. This is the law and the prophets." (Matt 7:12)

Reflection: The Golden Rule is recognized as a universal exhortation that transcends religion, culture, and time. Ancient religious and philosophical traditions, the Abrahamic religions (Judaism, Christianity, and Islam), many Eastern traditions, and even secular humanist traditions all share the belief Jesus expresses at the end of today's Gospel: "Do to others whatever you would have them do to you." So, if virtually every human community has asserted this for as long as we have written records, then why is it something we are so bad at doing?

The answer partly rests in our shared human tendency toward selfishness. Self-care and preservation are not, in themselves, bad instincts. Think, for example, of flight attendants' instructions to "put on your own oxygen mask before helping others" or the motto "You cannot give what you do not have." We must take care of ourselves in some basic ways in order to help others.

The problem arises when we attend to our needs without ever helping others with their "oxygen masks"—or without giving them the physical, emotional, or spiritual support they need. With his instruction to "ask and be given," "seek and find," "knock and be opened," Jesus is reminding us that love, help, and mercy are always readily available from God. Jesus frequently reminds us that our call is to be more like God in our words and deeds. When we ask something of God, God always provides, but when others need something from us, we often ignore. Perhaps the Golden Rule, then, is just a shorthand reminder to be more Godlike in our outlook and behavior.

Meditation: Jesus refers to the generosity parents naturally show their children. This is a reminder that most people are not absolutely selfish, but that we are often generous only to those closest to us. Are there ways I can expand my circle of generosity to live out the Golden Rule in my own life? Who do I resist treating as I would like to be treated?

Prayer: God of all grace, you give me everything I need and do not shy away from giving me more when I ask. Help me be more like you in the way I treat everyone I encounter, both the familiar and the stranger, those I like and those I struggle to appreciate.

Healing the Unseen Harm

Readings: Ezek 18:21-28; Matt 5:20-26

Scripture:
Is it my way that is unfair, or rather, are not your ways unfair?
(Ezek 18:25)

Reflection: One theme Jesus repeats throughout his public ministry is the impossibility of gauging a person's righteousness merely by their external appearance. This is why Jesus talks about dishes that appear clean on the outside but are rotted on the inside (Matt 23:25). It is also why he tells parables about wheat and weeds growing together, reminding his hearers that the "good" and the "bad" plants cannot be distinguished at first glance, but can only be separated at harvest time after they have fully grown.

Jesus challenges his followers to see a complex truth: our goodness and our sinfulness are both more than skin deep. This is why he says in today's Gospel that the ill will and anger we harbor in our hearts against others is also sinful. When we find ourselves in situations where we are holding on to anger or some other destructive attitude aimed at another person, it affects everything else in our lives. Experientially, we all know what this looks like—to be so angry at another, even if we don't acknowledge it out loud, that we cannot concentrate on other things in our lives. Jesus tells us to reconcile with that person and settle any other issues that have surfaced.

The prophet Ezekiel states plainly that those who turn away from sin and work to follow the will of God "shall surely live" and "shall not die." It's never too late to begin again, to do what we can to repair the harm we've caused in our relationships.

Meditation: It is difficult to maintain good, healthy relationships with others, even those we know and love very much. The hurt that comes with anger, frustration, disappointment, and jealousy is real, even if others may not understand or cannot see it. Where is there need for such healing in my own life? With whom do I need to make an effort toward reconciliation?

Prayer: Creator of life, you give us the wonderful and, at times, frightening ability to form relationships with others. Inspire in me the ability to work toward healing the broken relationships in my life and help me to see where I need to grow in my own ability to love, forgive, and reconcile.

The Tough Love of Christianity

Readings: Deut 26:16-19; Matt 5:43-48

Scripture:
"But I say to you, love your enemies . . ." (Matt 5:44)

Reflection: Jesus' command to love your enemies could not be plainer or more direct. Yet most of us do not hesitate to qualify or modify Jesus' otherwise simple instructions to suit our own situations. For example, even though we know Jesus tells us to love everyone, including those we view as enemies, there are often individuals or groups of people we decide not to include in this rule. "Yes, yes, Jesus said to love our enemies, but he surely wasn't talking about Osama bin Laden!" we might say. Or, "Yes, yes, Jesus said to love our enemies, but I don't think that applies to my sister-in-law!" We often make excuses and provide self-serving justifications to avoid following Jesus' admittedly challenging command.

But Jesus was fully aware of how difficult it is for us to do what God's will requires. In today's Gospel, Jesus draws a contrast between how we tend to live and how God wants us to live. It is not enough for us to love those we find easy to like and hate those we despise; we must love everyone as God has first loved us. Jesus knows this is challenging! Learning to take Jesus at his word without glossing over or qualifying his simple yet difficult teaching is part of our

Lenten journey. This season of penance and conversion is as good a time as any to practice what we say we believe as followers of Jesus Christ.

Meditation: Sin and selfishness often get in the way of authentically living the gospel life. We are often drawn to a comfortable lifestyle over the challenging demands of God's will. But what God expects of us is simple and uncomplicated: love. Who do I find difficult to love? When do I find myself introducing compromises or qualifications into the message of Jesus?

Prayer: Lord, you know how challenging it can be to follow the way you have set before us. I know I need to work on loving those I find difficult to love. Give me the strength to examine my own heart this Lent and strive to follow your will in all I say and do.

Learning to See Anew

Readings: Gen 15:5-12, 17-18; Phil 3:17–4:1 or 3:20–4:1; Luke 9:28b-36

Scripture:
While he was praying his face changed in appearance and his clothing became dazzling white. (Luke 9:29)

Reflection: The transfiguration is one of those well-known stories from the Gospels that does not often receive the deep reflection and consideration it deserves. Many of us assume that the transfiguration—when Jesus takes some of his closest followers up a mountain and something rather dramatic unfolds—is the unveiling of Jesus' full divinity. And this is certainly an understandable interpretation.

However, if we hold too closely to the idea that Jesus is pulling back part of the curtain to show some secret divinity, then we may start to veer into the theological territory of an ancient heresy known as "Docetism." This was the belief that Jesus Christ was merely "God in disguise" or that Jesus only "appeared" to be human. A modern way of describing this might be "Undercover Boss Christology"—a play on the popular TV show—where God is merely pretending to be like us but retains all the power and benefits of divinity with none of the risks and frailty of humanity.

But what if the transfiguration is less about what is happening to Jesus and more about what is happening to those who are with him? What if Jesus' followers are simply seeing him for who he actually is—seeing his full identity, his True Self?

At one point or another, we all struggle to recognize the fullness of one another's identities and goodness. Our failure to see ourselves and everyone else as beloved of God has led to so many forms of violence and dehumanization. What if we were able to see one another shining like the sun, transfigured before us, not as a result of some magical physical transformation, but because we have learned to see one another anew, to see each other as God sees us?

Meditation: One way to view the transfiguration is to see it as an invitation to look past surface appearances and judgments in order to recognize the beloved status of all God's children. What can I do today to see and love others differently?

Prayer: God of light, illuminate the darkness of my heart that I may see the radiance of your love in all creation. Help me love others as you have first loved us. Help me see the truth of each person's goodness and dignity.

Living the Mercy of God

Readings: Dan 9:4b-10; Luke 6:36-38

Scripture:
"Be merciful, just as your Father is merciful." (Luke 6:36)

Reflection: Sometimes Jesus' message is almost too simple, too direct, and too clear. It's often so uncomplicated that Christians just don't take it seriously. Such is the case with today's instruction from Jesus to his followers, where we are told to be merciful, to stop judging and condemning, and to forgive others so we also may be forgiven. So why don't we do as Jesus instructs?

I wonder if our resistance has to do with our inability to recognize and accept the love, forgiveness, mercy, and compassion that God continually bestows on us. The prophet Daniel reminds us in our first reading that God, despite our disobedience and selfishness, continues to keep God's side of the divine covenant with creation. We may be quick to walk away, to break our promises, to withhold mercy and justice from others. But God is steadfast.

In today's Gospel Jesus begins with a reminder that God is already merciful to us. Elsewhere Jesus teaches that God has already forgiven us our trespasses, yet we often remain obstinate in refusing others the same mercy. As we continue our Lenten journey, may we attune ourselves to recognizing and receiving the mercy and love that God has first shown to each of us, and may we strive to be signs of unity and instruments of peace to all we encounter.

Meditation: Sometimes baby steps are all we can manage. Learning to be merciful is not about jumping into some great heroic act of forgiveness but about embracing the chance to love one another in the small, simple opportunities that come our way each day. Where and with whom can I practice a small act of mercy today? How can forgiveness become a part of my Lenten practice?

Prayer: God of mercy, you know the hearts and minds of all your children. Open my heart so I may love like you. Heal my mind so I may recognize the many gifts you have given to me, so that I may share those gifts of love, mercy, justice, and peace with others.

Avoiding Hypocrisy

Readings: Isa 1:10, 16-20; Matt 23:1-12

Scripture:
"All their works are performed to be seen." (Matt 23:5)

Reflection: While Jesus is rightly remembered for his exercise of divine mercy and forgiveness, there is one form of sin that he consistently judges harshly throughout the Gospels: hypocrisy. Saying one thing and doing another, burdening others while being indifferent to their suffering, prioritizing one's own comfort while others struggle, claiming to be a person of faith and then using that religious tradition for self-aggrandizement—these are the sorts of things that Jesus simply cannot abide, especially when the transgressors are religious leaders.

We may not live in first-century Palestine or "widen [our] phylacteries and lengthen [our] tassels," but I'm certain that we all succumb to the temptation of hypocrisy now and then. We may claim to be followers of Christ, and then use our faith perspective as a tool to judge, discriminate against, or otherwise harm our neighbors. This is a form of hypocrisy, for Jesus repeatedly challenges us to love and forgive others. Still, so few self-identified Christians take Jesus' instructions on this matter seriously.

Granted, some people are more powerful and influential than you or me, and their responsibility to avoid hypocrisy is certainly greater. But that does not let us off the hook when it comes to examining our own consciences and reviewing how we might fall prey to the temptation to use religion as a means to our own ends or to justify dismissive or harmful behavior toward others. Jesus' message to us is clear: we must love, forgive, and, as Jesus notes in today's Gospel, *serve* one another as God has already done for us.

Meditation: How do I relate to my faith tradition? Do I see it as a divine resource to guide me toward being a better person and neighbor to all? Or do I see it as a set of rules and standards by which I judge, dismiss, or even harm others? Where can I grow in being a better servant of God through service to others?

Prayer: God of authenticity, you call us to walk the talk we profess in following you. Your son Jesus showed us the path, preached to us the way, and modeled the manner of authentic faith and action. Give me the courage to live what I profess in word and deed.

Knowing the Right Thing to Do

Readings: 2 Sam 7:4-5a, 12-14a, 16; Rom 4:13, 16-18, 22; Matt 1:16, 18-21, 24a or Luke 2:41-51a

Scripture:
Joseph her husband, since he was a righteous man, yet unwilling to expose her to shame, decided to divorce her quietly. (Matt 1:19)

Reflection: The story of Jesus' conception and birth is interesting from almost every angle. With its account of a pregnancy, angels, dreams, and more, there's a whole novel's worth of drama in just a few verses of Scripture! It is understandable, then, that we might focus our attention on the miraculous pregnancy or direct our energy toward the ultimate protagonist of the story, Jesus. But to do so might mean unwittingly overlooking another insight that unfolds in Matthew's account of the birth of Jesus.

The figure of Joseph, the earthly father of Jesus, is often an afterthought when it comes to the Holy Family or even Christianity in general. He is rightly venerated for not abandoning Mary in the wake of her pregnancy, and tradition holds that he was a loving father to Jesus. However, in this important Gospel story, we find another aspect of Joseph that is relatable and important. Here we encounter a person of integrity and dignity, someone who finds himself in a personal situation that is confusing and embarrassing, who is seeking desperately to do the right thing.

Even though the thought of separating from Mary seems terrible to us, Joseph's intention is to uphold Mary's inherent dignity and value. Eventually an angel reveals God's intention for the couple, but even before this, we are told that Joseph is committed to trying to do what is right.

Joseph's story is a reminder to all of us about the importance of careful discernment and the true intentions behind our actions. We may not have immediate answers or arrive at correct conclusions on our own, but the desire to do what is right is always a good start.

Meditation: When I find myself in difficult or unexpected circumstances, what informs my intentions? What motivates my actions? Do I strive to do what is right and uphold the dignity of others? Or am I more inclined to put myself, my interests, or my desires first?

Prayer: God of discernment, you built on Joseph's good intentions and helped him see your will for him and his future family. Inspire in me a desire to always do the right thing, and give me the insight to recognize how you are guiding me.

Don't Choose Ignorance

Readings: Jer 17:5-10; Luke 16:19-31

Scripture:
"They have Moses and the prophets. Let them listen to them."
(Luke 16:29)

Reflection: There are few stories in the Gospels more terrifying than that of Lazarus and the rich man. At least, it *should* be terrifying for all who embrace a kind of willful ignorance of the suffering of others while striving to preserve their own comfort and security.

Names are important in the Bible, which is why it's no accident that the wealthy man doesn't receive one and the poor man does. Jesus is flipping the social and cultural expectations about importance and value upside down. The hearers in Jesus' time would have expected the wealthy man to be named and Lazarus to be an anonymous background character—dismissed as disposable and insignificant, undeserving of a name. But as Jesus proclaims through word and deed, God's way of seeing the world is not our way of seeing the world. Indeed, the prophets consistently repeat that God is on the side of the poor and the vulnerable.

The rich man's sin is the active choice he made, even in the afterlife, to embrace ignorance for the sake of his own comfort. He didn't want to know about the plight of Lazarus and others like him. The rich man had the information, resources, and agency to change his ways and do what was right, but instead, he chose to "not know" at every turn.

Today, there are lots of people like the rich man who live comfortable, secure, and stable lives. We need not be billionaires for Jesus' story to apply to us. And if we choose this type of ignorance, then this story should terrify us, too.

Meditation: What realities am I afraid to face in the world and community around me? Do I intentionally shield myself from the suffering of others? What can I do to open my eyes to those in need and respond as Christ calls me?

Prayer: God of justice, you call us to hear the cry of the poor and to respond as you would, with generosity and love. Help me to be more like Christ in how I see the world and to selflessly support those around me who are in need.

Envy that Kills

Readings: Gen 37:3-4, 12-13a, 17b-28a; Matt 21:33-43, 45-46

Scripture:
[T]hey hated him so much that they would not even greet him. (Gen 37:4)

Reflection: Envy is a powerful and destructive force that leads to sorrow, anger, hatred, and even violence. The story of Joseph being sold into slavery by his brothers because they were jealous of their father's love is disturbing on several levels: the initial plan to kill Joseph before they abandon him and then trade him to nomadic people, the human trafficking of a child, the total disregard for the safety of another person, and the dramatic failure of familial love. But as extreme and exceptional as the details of this story are, the experience of envy—including jealousy among siblings and other family members—is familiar to us all.

Envy, counted among the "seven deadly sins," is the feeling of competition with one's peers. It leads to a spirit of covetousness, ill will toward others, and a sense of inferiority. Envy can motivate us to knock others down, to boost our own egos, to minimize the success or happiness of others in a pathetic effort to alleviate our own sense of inadequacy. In some extreme cases, as in the stories of Joseph's brothers or

Cain, the brother of Abel, envy can lead to violence or even murder.

As common as envy is, it is nevertheless something that God wants us to overcome. This is why envy (or "covetousness") appears in two of the Ten Commandments (Exod 20:17) and why Jesus spends so much of his ministry preaching and demonstrating that each of us is already fully loved by God.

This Lent is a good time to evaluate where envy lies in our hearts and behaviors, and then do something about it. God wants us to be free of this heavy burden.

Meditation: Are there people or things that trigger a sense of competition or lead me to think less of myself? Do I wish the downfall or harm of others? Am I ready to surrender these thoughts and feelings to God?

Prayer: God of unending love, you desire that each of us experience the fullness of joy. Help me to be a less envious person and to accept the divine gifts of love and grace you always bestow on me.

There's More to the Story

Readings: Mic 7:14-15, 18-20; Luke 15:1-3, 11-32

Scripture:
So to them Jesus addressed this parable. "A man had two
sons . . ." (Luke 15:11)

Reflection: There is perhaps no better illustration of a dysfunctional family in the New Testament than the one in the
parable of the Prodigal Son. I have long thought that this
story is misunderstood by our typical commonsense interpretation, which goes something like this: the younger son
is selfish and greedy but has a change of heart and returns
home asking for forgiveness; the father is generous and loving to both sons; and the older son is envious and bitter about
how the younger son is treated.

But, the way I read it, there are no clear heroes or any
actual signs of conversion in the story. The younger son is
without a doubt selfish. His return home appears to be about
utility, survival, and comfort. He never takes responsibility
for his actions; he simply rehearses a set of lines describing
what he thinks will sound good, and then delivers them
verbatim. The father does not seem to have a good relationship with either of his children, as seen both in the way the
younger son relates to him and in his inability to reach the
older son. The older son is certainly embittered, but it is not

unreasonable given the circumstances, and his relationships with his father and brother are both deeply frayed. This could be anybody's family at any time in history.

Jesus purposefully leaves the story open-ended so we can reflect on how each of the three family members might better relate to and love one another. Jesus' parable is both a thought experiment and an examination of conscience, inviting us to place ourselves in the shoes of one or more of the characters, to consider our own relationships, judgments, and behaviors, and to grow in awareness of our own need for genuine conversion.

Meditation: Family dynamics can be difficult to navigate. Knowing people so well can lead to uniquely complicated feelings. What dynamics do I need to work on in my own family relationships this Lent?

Prayer: God, you invite us to imagine you as a parent, as our Father or Mother (Ps 103:13; Isa 66:13). Help us to be better members of our earthly families and to reflect to one another the divine love you show us.

The True Name of God

Readings: Exod 3:1-8a, 13-15; 1 Cor 10:1-6, 10-12; Luke 13:1-9

Scripture:
"This is my name . . . thus am I to be remembered through all generations." (Exod 3:15)

Reflection: As a child, the story of God speaking to Moses through the burning bush captured my imagination. The story itself was fascinating, and the visualization of it in Cecil B. DeMille's film *The Ten Commandments* was spectacular. As time went on, my fascination with a non-consuming fire waned and was replaced with increasing interest in what I considered to be the philosophical message of the story. God's name—"I AM"—became the riddle to be solved, the mystery that begged to be understood in order to understand who God truly is. But in time I learned that I, like many others, was getting distracted by the wrong part of God's message.

The name of God is not a philosophical enigma. God's name is *relationship*. It's true that God tells Moses to say that "I AM" sent him, but if we stop there, we miss the bigger reveal. God goes on to say that the one who sends Moses is the God of the Israelites, the God who hears the injustice they experience now, the God who loves them, knows them, is with them, and will be with them as they go forward. I once heard a Scripture scholar say that "I AM" is more accurately rendered as "I am the One who will be there with you." And the late Catholic theologian Catherine Mowry LaCugna expressed this divine name as "God for us."

Today's first reading does help us know who God is, but it also reveals how God relates to us: as the one who accompanies us, understands our struggles, and desires only the best for our futures.

Meditation: The true name of God reveals not only who God is but how God acts in the world. God created us to be in relationship with one another, with God, and with all creation. To love as God loves us is to love one another. Where do I need to be more Godlike in my life today?

Prayer: God of love, through your exchange with Moses you reveal that you are all about relationship. Help me to better imitate you by loving others and being present to the people in my life. Just as you are always there for us, give me the strength to be there for others.

Embracing the Prophetic Call

Readings: 2 Kgs 5:1-15b; Luke 4:24-30

Scripture:
"[N]o prophet is accepted in his own native place." (Luke 4:24)

Reflection: Throughout the Old Testament, nearly every prophet called to proclaim the word of God tried to get out of the responsibility. These would-be prophets understood that accepting God's call meant accepting a certain degree of risk and rejection.

To be a prophet is to announce the disparity between how we are living as a society and how God wants us to live, particularly when the wealthy and powerful are benefitting from the suffering and oppression of the poor and marginalized. Announcing the gap between these two realities is risky because it unsettles the comfortable and demands concrete social change.

Being a prophet is not about predicting the future or having an original idea. Rather, it is about bearing God's righteous news, which is good news for the poor and weak, and often disturbing news for the wealthy and powerful. For this reason, Jesus can say as a simple matter of fact that "no prophet is accepted in his own native place." Not only do prophets face social pressure to be silenced, but they are also usually dismissed by those who have known them earlier in life.

Those who are closest to us—our friends, siblings, neighbors, coworkers—are often so familiar to us that we know their weaknesses and imperfections. Relying on our knowledge or assumptions, we may be quick to ignore or reject difficult truths they convey, even if they are correct and the message is from God.

Meditation: When do I find myself relativizing, dismissing, or contesting hard truths others challenge me to see? Are there times when I find myself ignored or rejected when relaying a difficult message to those who know me well? What do I need to do to better hear the prophets in my life and proclaim God's message to others?

Prayer: God of the prophets, you call people in every generation to announce good news to the poor and challenging news to the powerful. Inspire in me the confidence to announce your vision of peace in difficult times and places, and help me to hear the prophetic message you proclaim to me through others.

Not an Easy Decision

Readings: Isa 7:10-14; 8:10; Heb 10:4-10; Luke 1:26-38

Scripture:
But she was greatly troubled at what was said . . . (Luke 1:29)

Reflection: When thinking about the solemnity of the Annunciation, I am reminded of the ways we contemporary Christians so often breeze past the details in the story. We already know what happens to Mary and Joseph and Jesus. But as the scene between the angel Gabriel and Mary unfolds in today's Gospel, let's slow down and reflect on what is revealed to us in Scripture. If we allow ourselves to attend to the story as it unfolds, as if hearing it for the first time, new details and inspiration can surface.

For example, did you ever stop to think about how scared Mary is in today's Gospel? Mary is terrified. She is described by Luke as "greatly troubled" and is so disturbed that the angel even has to say, "Do not be afraid, Mary." In addition to the confusion wrought by conceiving a child without having had a sexual relationship, Mary is also confronted with fears of social shame and religious stigma, worries about her relationship with Joseph, and concerns about what any of this means. Mary doesn't say "yes" right away. It takes some explaining by the angel and some time for her to grapple with the magnitude of what is being asked of her.

If we skip over the details of Mary's experience because we already have the benefit of knowing "how the story ends," then we miss how much Mary is just like the rest of us. It can be scary to say "yes" to God and to do what we know is right, especially when what is right is hard.

Meditation: Mary's experience and example remind us that doing God's will can be deeply challenging, and that saying "yes" to God can be scary. What are the ways God is asking me to change or to act differently? Does this frighten me? How does Mary's example bring me comfort or direction?

Prayer: God of life, you called Mary to embrace a challenging but important role in salvation history. Help me overcome my fear and say "yes" to doing your will. May I be like Mary and do my part in working for the kingdom of God.

Not Forgetting the Small Signs of God

Readings: Deut 4:1, 5-9; Matt 5:17-19

Scripture:
"[T]ake care and be earnestly on your guard not to forget the things which your own eyes have seen . . ." (Deut 4:9)

Reflection: Most of us, when thinking about Moses leading the Israelites out of captivity in Egypt, recall extraordinary acts of divine intervention. We might think of parting seas or pillars of flame or the ten plagues. These signs are both spectacular and memorable. But the words of Moses in today's first reading suggest that, years into their journey to the Promised Land, some memories are beginning to fade among God's people. Even the source of their life, freedom, and hope—God—is slowly being forgotten or ignored.

The fact that Moses brings up the importance of memory at the end of an exhortation about observing the statutes and decrees of the covenant suggests that such practices help us recall the very source and ground of our life and freedom. While most of us will never experience anything close to the oppression of the Israelites in Egypt, all of us share a common source of liberation in God. That any of us exist—that anything exists at all—is thanks to the God of creation who sustains us in every moment of our lives. And yet we can be so quick to ignore or forget that basic, essential fact.

Practices like observing God's commandments, keeping the Sabbath holy, praying regularly, and caring for those at the margins are not merely ends in themselves. Through those acts of love and mercy, we are invited to reflect on God as the source of all that is good and holy in our lives. Perhaps this is why Jesus was so keen to defend the law. He recognized its important and instructive role in the lives of God's people.

Meditation: As our Lenten journey continues, may we see our fidelity to the commands God has given us as an opportunity for reflection and gratitude. How might I better attend to the divine presence in my life?

Prayer: God of freedom, you heard the cries of your people in Egypt and led them out of bondage to new life. Help me remember that you are the source of my life and all that is. Strengthen me to be faithful to your commandments.

Hearing the Prophets of Our Time

Readings: Jer 7:23-28; Luke 11:14-23

Scripture:
"I will be your God and you shall be my people." (Jer 7:23)

Reflection: In Scripture, God is often described as a parent. Of course, we know that the way God thinks, acts, and loves far exceeds that of even the greatest of human parents. But if God were like a human parent, we might imagine that God would be endlessly frustrated by our shenanigans, disobedience, and unnecessary drama. This sense of "divine frustration" comes through in Jeremiah's message to the people. Jeremiah lays out the divine agenda quite clearly: listen to God's voice; do what's right; then God will be our God, and we will be God's people. Simple!

And yet God appears to lament the fact that the people ignore not only God's instructions, but also the reminders provided by generations of prophets. God is warning Jeremiah that although Jeremiah has an important message to deliver, it is unlikely that his audience will take heed. God calls the people "the nation that does not listen."

What about us? Are we any different than Jeremiah's audience? Are we part of a people that is willing to listen to the hard truths and difficult messages delivered by God's prophets in our time? All we need to do is look around our society and even our church to see a community of people who are divided, angry, fearful, and frustrated. Selfishness takes hold when lack of trust in God and neighbor increases.

As believers, we often say we want to be God's people and do God's will, but our actions often speak much louder than our words. Let us attend to the cries for justice and peace in our midst, and care for the poor and the earth. Let us heed the messages God proclaims through contemporary prophets, those religious and secular voices that announce what is ours to do.

Meditation: What fears occupy my mind and heart that close me to the difficult truths God is speaking to me today? How can I better hear God through contemporary prophets?

Prayer: God of love and justice, for generations you have reminded us through the oracles of your prophets what it means to be your people. Help me hear your voice and respond to the prophetic call to do your will, so I can be yours and you can be my God.

The God of Mercy

Readings: Hos 14:2-10; Mark 12:28-34

Scripture:
Return, O Israel, to the LORD, your God . . . (Hos 14:2)

Reflection: One of the most striking elements of Pope Francis's ministry as Bishop of Rome has been his commitment to reminding the faithful of God's inexhaustible mercy. It's not hard to see why he has made mercy the centerpiece of his pastoral mission. Both the prophets in the Old Testament and Jesus Christ in the New Testament constantly bear witness to the mercy of God. But do we recognize it? Do we believe in divine mercy, love, and forgiveness?

In April 2013, when Pope Francis officially took possession of the Chair of Peter in Rome, he preached: "God's patience has to call forth in us the courage to return to him, however many mistakes and sins there may be in our life." He added: "Maybe someone among us here is thinking: my sin is so great, I am as far from God as the younger son in the parable, my unbelief is like that of Thomas; I don't have the courage to go back, to believe that God can welcome me and that he is waiting for me, of all people. But God is indeed waiting for you; he asks of you only the courage to go to him."

This is also the message of God proclaimed by the prophet Hosea. All God asks of us is to return to God, regardless of how far afield we have gone, how sinful we have been, or how undeserving we feel. God is there, always, patiently waiting, longing for us to turn around and be embraced by the love and mercy that only God can show.

Meditation: So many of us do not believe we are worthy of God's love and mercy, that our absence from church or our life choices or the mistakes we have made make us ineligible for God's embrace. What is preventing me from turning to God now, at this moment, and accepting God's love and mercy?

Prayer: God of mercy, you never turn away from any of your children. You have communicated through your prophets and your Son that you want us to return to you, to embrace your love and forgiveness, and to live life to the fullest. Give me the grace to turn to you.

What Does God Really Want?

Readings: Hos 6:1-6; Luke 18:9-14

Scripture:
For it is love that I desire, not sacrifice,
  and knowledge of God rather than burnt offerings.
    (Hos 6:6)

Reflection: What does God want from me? If you are like me, this is a question you find yourself asking from time to time. It might arise because of some frustration or disappointment in life. It might arise out of a desire to be a better person or a better follower of Christ. Whatever the circumstances, the question tends to haunt us until we come to some conclusion.

Today's Gospel presents us with two possible responses to this question. Jesus tells a story about two people going to the temple to pray: one is a self-righteous Pharisee and the other is a tax collector who is understood to be a cheat. From the outside, it appears the Pharisee is doing everything right. He seems to know exactly what God wants from him and, therefore, from others. He's also convinced that he is better at doing what God wants than others are. Meanwhile, the tax collector approaches God with great self-awareness and humility. He knows he is a sinner—imperfect and in need of improvement. The tax collector is not convinced that merely saying the right words in formal prayer or offering burnt offerings at the temple is sufficient because his own examination of conscience reveals the need for ongoing conversion.

The divine word in today's reading from Hosea resonates with Jesus' story of the two men at prayer. What God wants from us is rather simple: God wants us to love and know God and, by extension, to love and know one another. Sadly, the Pharisee in Jesus' story doesn't seem to know or love God, his tax-collector neighbor, or even himself. He is much farther from answering the question of what God truly wants.

Meditation: What God wants from us is a deeper relationship in love. How do I answer the question of what God wants from me right now? How might I become more like the tax collector in my prayer and actions?

Prayer: God of humility and love, you draw near through your Son Jesus Christ and show us the way of peace and community. Give me the courage and the humility to love you and know you, to love my neighbor and know my neighbor, and to love myself and know myself.

Ecological Prodigal Children

Readings: Josh 5:9a, 10-12; 2 Cor 5:17-21; Luke 15:1-3, 11-32

Scripture:
"[T]he younger son collected all his belongings and set off to a distant country where he squandered his inheritance on a life of dissipation." (Luke 15:13)

Reflection: This is the second time we hear the parable of the Prodigal Son proclaimed during the Lenten season. When we revisit a biblical passage during the same liturgical season, it is a sign that the text is important and that it may provide us with a deeper meaning than we at first assumed. This is certainly the case with this story, one of the most famous of Jesus' parables.

It is common for us to think about the human dynamics in the story of this admittedly dysfunctional family. But what if we were to consider the dynamics of this family on a cosmic scale? What if we imagined the father character as a stand-in for what Pope Francis calls "our common home" or St. Francis of Assisi calls "our Sister Mother Earth"? Perhaps then we might find ourselves, as a species and community, in the position of the younger son, but in a new context.

Scripture and tradition remind us that we belong to one divine family of creation. God loves into existence the whole cosmos, which is interconnected and interdependent. Although the created world has been particularly good at giving us what we need to survive as human creatures, we have been rapacious in our taking of plant and animal life, while also polluting the planet with a disregard that reflects the younger son's disregard for his father and family. Like the younger son, we continually want more when we have squandered even the excess we've already taken. On this cosmic scale, the rest of creation is much like the older son, always doing its part while witnessing our destructive behavior.

How might we change this story?

Meditation: Both Pope St. John Paul II and Pope Francis have invited us to embrace "ecological conversion," to change our outlook, practices, and our relationship with the rest of creation. What more can we learn about ecological conversion from the dynamics of this parable?

Prayer: God of creation, you love all that exists into being. Open our eyes to our human selfishness and ecological sinfulness so we may change our ways and take our place within your family of creation.

Known Too Well

Readings: Isa 65:17-21; John 4:43-54

Scripture:
"Unless you people see signs and wonders, you will not believe." (John 4:48)

Reflection: When we focus exclusively on the divinity of Jesus and minimize his humanity, we can miss some of the social and familial dynamics he experienced. One of these dynamics, attested to in all four Gospels, is the fact that his preaching and ministry were not well received by those who knew him best in his hometown. Today's Gospel passage from John begins with this acknowledgement: "For Jesus himself testified that a prophet has no honor in his native place." In Mark's account we are told that Jesus couldn't do much in Nazareth by way of miracles because of the resistance he faced there (6:5). In Matthew's account we hear about how those who knew Jesus were offended by his preaching and ministry (13:57). And in Luke's account, the townspeople drove him out of the synagogue and tried to throw him down a hill (4:29)!

I would guess that everyone has, at one time or another, had an experience like Jesus. Perhaps it's being affirmed in your workplace but unappreciated by family members. Perhaps it's having your opinion valued by acquaintances but disregarded by those who know you well. Those who know us best also know us at our worst. They recall when we have messed up or made poor decisions. They can form judgments about who we are and what we are capable of, preventing them from seeing us in all our complexity and goodness.

We have also been on the other side of this situation: we can pigeonhole others, too! When we doubt someone can change, when we disregard a good idea or opinion, we are committing the same error as those who reject Jesus. God is working in and through those around us, even those we know well.

Meditation: Who are those people close to me that I write off, dismiss, or reject on account of my opinion of them? Do I allow my opinions of others to change and develop with time, or do I assume the way I view them is absolute?

Prayer: God of all life, your Holy Spirit continues to draw near to empower and inspire all people and all creation. Help me have an open heart and mind. Give me the humility and courage to recognize the many ways people can and do change.

When God Surprises Us

Readings: Ezek 47:1-9, 12; John 5:1-16

Scripture:
Come! behold the deeds of the LORD,
   the astounding things he has wrought on earth. (Ps 46:9)

Reflection: There are two types of people in this world: those who like to be surprised and those who don't. I fall into the latter category. I have always disliked surprise birthday parties or other unexpected events, even when the orchestrator of the surprise is well-meaning and the gesture is kind. So, while I would like to think that my response to Jesus' actions in today's Gospel would be positive, the surprise that throws off his contemporaries and turns some of them into adversaries causes me to reflect a little more deeply.

That Jesus healed a man who had been ill for almost forty years is itself surprising, but the fact that he performed this act of mercy on the Sabbath was a bridge too far for some in the community. The Gospel tells us that these critics of Jesus were so upset that they wanted to kill him (5:18)! What was so upsetting about this amazing act of generosity and healing? At the heart of this rage against Jesus was likely the fear of his disrupting the status quo and challenging conventional thinking about God and the world.

Those who recognize the power of God working in and through Jesus can see this healing miracle as another sign of divine love and mercy. But for those who like things to be predictable, understandable, and even controllable, this action was a very unwelcome surprise. On that level, I can relate to the initial emotions of those who were angry with Jesus, even if I completely disagree with their actions. And that challenges me to reconsider how I respond when God surprises me.

Meditation: How tightly do I hold on to my understanding and expectations for how God can act in my life and in the world? Do I get upset when things don't go as I planned? Are there ways God may be working in my life and in the lives of those around me that I don't understand or refuse to accept?

Prayer: God of surprises, you break through the predictable pattern of our lives to inspire, challenge, and heal. Help me welcome your unconditional love and mercy, especially when it is unexpected.

April 2: Wednesday of the Fourth Week of Lent

Who Is Jesus?

Readings: Isa 49:8-15; John 5:17-30

Scripture:
"I do not seek my own will but the will of the one who sent me." (John 5:30)

Reflection: Each of the four Gospels gives us a particular glimpse at the identity and mission of Jesus Christ. While it can be confusing to see variation among the Gospel accounts, the blessing of this rich variety is that through it we can gain greater appreciation for who Jesus is. For example, in the Gospel of Matthew we see the connections Jesus has to his Jewish heritage and the great prophets and leaders of the past. The Gospel of Luke bears special witness to Jesus' teaching and preaching, especially through parables found only in Luke's account.

Today we get a clear look at how the Gospel of John presents who Jesus is and what it means for us. The last line in John's prologue gives us an important clue for how to interpret Jesus' identity throughout this Gospel: "No one has ever seen God. The only Son, God, who is at the Father's side, has revealed him" (John 1:18). The Gospel tells us from the outset that Jesus is identified with God, so close to the Father that he is able to reveal the fullness of divinity through his words and deeds.

Today's passage builds on this revelation. Jesus tells his followers that he is not some independent contractor or rogue actor, but someone who is single-mindedly focused on doing the will of God. Everything he says, everything he desires, every miracle he performs—*everything* comes from God. In other words, if you want to know what God is like, look at Jesus!

John's Gospel fully acknowledges Jesus' humanity but emphasizes that Jesus is also divine. We should remember this when seeking to do God's will: Jesus has already shown us the way.

Meditation: Who do I say Jesus is? There are abundant images, stories, and encounters in the Gospels that reveal glimpses of Jesus' identity and mission. What surprises me today about who Jesus truly is?

Prayer: God of relationship, you entered the world as one of us to draw near to our experiences, our joys, and our struggles. Help me see in the life and teachings of Jesus Christ the way to live your will.

What Motivates You?

Readings: Exod 32:7-14; John 5:31-47

Scripture:
"I do not accept human praise . . ." (John 5:41)

Reflection: The ego is a challenging thing. On the one hand, we all need well established identities that distinguish us from one another and help us develop appropriate interpersonal boundaries. On the other hand, our focus on ourselves can devolve into self-centeredness, a spirit of individualism, and a desire to be personally affirmed at all costs. It's likely that we've all faced the temptation to dwell on ourselves, inflate our sense of importance based on the approval or praise of others, or indulge a sense of grievance when such approval or praise is withheld.

In today's Gospel Jesus speaks about what motivates him. He states plainly that his preaching, teaching, and healings are not about his own self-aggrandizement, nor does this mission and ministry originate with him. Instead, it is God who calls him to perform these great works, and it is God who is the source of Jesus' confidence and assurance. We can see this motivation play out through the entirety of Jesus' earthly ministry, but especially in the last days before his crucifixion.

When Jesus is betrayed, denied, reviled, humiliated, and tortured for merely loving others as God has loved him and calling all of us to do likewise, we clearly see the "testimony" or witness of his motivation. The challenge for us as we continue on our Lenten journey is to examine what motivates *us*. Is it God's will or something else?

Meditation: When we make decisions about what to do or say, we are often faced with conflicting values and motivations. How much does God's will and Jesus' example influence my thoughts, judgments, and behaviors? Where can I grow during this Lent to become more Christlike in my motives and identity?

Prayer: Lord Jesus, you followed the will of God in all you said and did. Give me the grace to be more like you in thought and deed, seeking not the approval or praise of others, but the single-hearted desire to do what God is asking of me.

Don't Be a "Nice Guy"

Readings: Wis 2:1a, 12-22; John 7:1-2, 10, 25-30

Scripture:
"Let us beset the just one, because he is obnoxious to us . . ."
(Wis 2:12)

Reflection: Jesus was not a nice guy. At first glance, it may seem like I'm insulting our Lord, but that is not my intention! By "nice guy," I am referring to someone who doesn't "rock the boat," who doesn't make others uncomfortable by drawing attention to injustice, who chooses to remain silent rather than speak up. A "nice guy" is someone who, to borrow a phrase from yesterday's Gospel, prefers to "accept human praise" (John 5:41).

In this sense, Jesus would hardly be considered a "nice guy" because he clearly upset the status quo and definitely "rocked the boat" of the establishment. He didn't lob insults or incite violence; he preached nothing but the love of God and neighbor. However, that was enough for those threatened by his preaching and ministry to do exactly what the book of Wisdom describes in today's first reading. Written centuries before the birth of Jesus, this meditation on the mindset of people who wish to silence those they find "obnoxious" describes Jesus' situation well.

To not be a "nice guy" doesn't mean becoming a bad or mean person. It means not letting fear of what others think, or the temptation to appease the powerful at the expense of the suffering, or the desire to be liked, prevent us from living the gospel wholeheartedly. Discipleship is not always easy, and it sometimes comes with uncomfortable consequences. This is something worth reflecting on in our final weeks of Lent.

Meditation: Like many of the Hebrew prophets and John the Baptist, Jesus paid the ultimate price for announcing the kingdom of God and following the divine will in his preaching, teaching, and healing ministry. As I strive to live as an authentic disciple of Christ, where do I need to grow in becoming more Christlike, regardless of the consequences?

Prayer: God of courage, you never abandon us but always accompany us in our journey through life. Strengthen me to accept the call of discipleship, to do what is right, and to announce the good news with my whole life, even when it may cost me my comfort or my reputation.

What Would Jesus Do?

Readings: Jer 11:18-20; John 7:40-53

Scripture:
Let me witness the vengeance you take on them,
   for to you I have entrusted my cause! (Jer 11:20)

Reflection: The theme of facing consequences for being a prophet continues in today's readings. In our first reading, Jeremiah reflects on the growing resistance that rises in response to his preaching the word of God. Earlier, God had called Jeremiah and told him, in response to his initial protest, that God would guide him and tell him what he needed to proclaim. So Jeremiah began his divinely commissioned ministry. In response, those in power immediately felt threatened and began plotting to silence him.

In response to the pushback, threats, and anger he experienced as result of his prophetic ministry, Jeremiah exhibits a common desire felt by those who face opposition or attack: he wants revenge! While this may be a perfectly natural feeling, it is nevertheless contrary to God's desire for how we are meant to live. We know this because God incarnate in Jesus Christ shows us how we are meant to respond.

Not seeking retribution for the harm done to us, especially in times when we are sincerely striving to do the right thing, is one of the greatest challenges for those of us who are affected by sin. But Jesus' example of what it means to be fully human challenges our gut instinct to inflict pain for pain, to demand an "eye for an eye." Jesus reveals to us that violence and vengeance are never the answer; rather, they are the perpetuation of injustice and the opposite of how God calls us to live.

Meditation: The prophets were not immune from the desire for retribution and revenge—feelings we know all too well. What are the ways I find myself lashing out in thought, word, or deed against those who have attacked me? When others malign or dismiss me, what is my response? How is God calling me to respond in the face of hatred?

Prayer: God of justice, you know us better than we know ourselves, so you understand our temptation to return hatred for hatred. Help me to see others as you see them, and give me the patience to be more Christlike toward those who wish me ill.

We Are All Sinners, Too

Readings: Isa 43:16-21; Phil 3:8-14; John 8:1-11

Scripture:
[S]ee, I am doing something new!
   Now it springs forth, do you not perceive it? (Isa 43:19)

Reflection: Jesus' preaching and ministry can be viewed as an exercise in challenging authority. The authority in question is not that of God, for God's will is the only authority that matters to Jesus. Instead, Jesus regularly questions the authority of conventional logic, group thinking, and religious hypocrisy.

In today's Gospel, we see this dynamic play out in Jesus' encounter with the woman accused of adultery. Here we see Jesus challenging three kinds of authority: the conventional logic about how to deal with people who commit seemingly grave offenses, the group thinking that could lead the crowd to pick up stones in anticipation of executing this alleged sinner, and the dubious leadership of religious authorities who are primarily interested in entrapping Jesus rather than in the life and safety of the woman before them.

But Jesus is having none of it. He doesn't engage any of these people directly. He refuses to play their game or enter into public debate. Instead, he merely waits them out and then presents the one line that uncovers all forms of hypocrisy: "Let the one among you who is without sin be the first to throw a stone at her."

It can be easy to reduce this scene to an instance of "love the sinner, hate the sin." But that interpretation doesn't do justice to the profound examination of conscience Jesus presents to us. The point is that *everybody* is a sinner. None of us is worthy to throw a stone, real or proverbial, at another person because each of us, in our own way, has sinned and continues to sin. The instruction to "go and sin no more" is as much for each of us as it is for this one woman.

Meditation: For most of us, it is easy to point the finger at another, judge their sinfulness, and walk away feeling superior. But Jesus challenges us to look instead at our own hearts and behaviors. Will I accept his challenge?

Prayer: God of truth, give me the grace to examine my life and recognize the ways I sin against you in the way I treat myself, others, and creation.

April 7: Monday of the Fifth Week of Lent

A Light that Guides and Changes Us

Readings: Dan 13:1-9, 15-17, 19-30, 33-62 or 13:41c-62; John 8:12-20

Scripture:
"I am the light of the world." (John 8:12)

Reflection: Light is such an interesting image in today's Gospel, as Jesus refers to himself as "the light of the world." Light can be understood literally, as in the rays of the sun or the bright ambience of a stoked fireplace, but it can also be understood metaphorically, as in the illumination of one's mind or the presentation of a bright idea. Light provides direction and perspective, and it allows for learning and insight.

Both conceptions of light serve as useful metaphors as we think about how Jesus functions in our lives. He is, as he says elsewhere in the Gospel of John, "the way and the truth and the life" (John 14:6). Jesus is the key to knowing where to go as he lights our way, and he helps us understand what is good and true through the illumination of our minds.

As we get closer to the great Easter Vigil, it's helpful to recall how that sacred liturgy begins in almost total darkness. With the lighting of a fire, the blessing of a candle, and the sharing of flame, our ability to see around us grows, and changes how we relate to our surroundings. Shortly thereafter we hear the wisdom of Scripture proclaimed, illuminating our minds and hearts, changing how we think about ourselves, the world, and God. Christ is a light that guides and changes us—showing us the way, showing us who we are called to be.

Meditation: Reflecting on the metaphor of light, what guides me in my life journey? Do I move through life as one stumbling in the dark? Do I look to Christ to illuminate my path and my mind, or do I turn to other sources or guides?

Prayer: Creator of light, you sent the Eternal Word to show us the way and to guide our path through life. Help me turn to Christ for direction, and lead me where you want me to go.

Are We There Yet?

Readings: Num 21:4-9; John 8:21-30

Scripture:
But with their patience worn out by the journey, the people complained against God and Moses . . . (Num 21:4-5)

Reflection: "Are we there yet?" What parent on a long family road trip hasn't heard that phrase uttered from the mouth of a child in the back seat? Boredom, frustration, and restlessness set in—with whining and complaining not far behind—as the journey drags on. This impatience is the sort of attitude that comes to mind when I think about the scene from the book of Numbers in our first reading today.

God, through Moses, has led the chosen people out of captivity in Egypt, but the journey toward the Promised Land is taking a very long time. Or at least it's taking far longer than the people would like. According to Scripture, God becomes frustrated with the complaints of the people of Israel and—in what might be considered an extreme example of "I'm going to turn this car around!"—punishes the complainers with an infestation of poisonous serpents. Although God eventually relents in response to the people's acknowledgement that they were wrong to complain, I still read it as a bit of a divine overreaction!

Nevertheless, there are several themes this story raises that are especially worth considering on our own journeys this Lent. For example, how do we react when things don't go according to our preferred timeline? Do we complain like frustrated children on a road trip, or do we take time to reflect on how we can better trust in God? This Lenten season is a good time to reflect on these sorts of questions and to grow, as children do, in patience and trust.

Meditation: Like the people of Israel, each of us can find ourselves frustrated, impatient, and angry about situations that do not go as planned. Where might I need to grow in patience with God and others? How can I use the remaining time of Lent to develop deeper trust in God?

Prayer: Creator of time, it can be difficult to maintain faith when things do not seem to align with our expectations or hopes. Give me the grace to trust in you and to recognize you as the source of my strength and hope.

Cheap or Costly Grace?

Readings: Dan 3:14-20, 91-92, 95; John 8:31-42

Scripture:
"If our God, whom we serve, can save us . . . may he save us! But even if he will not, know, O king, that we will not serve your god . . ." (Dan 3:17-18)

Reflection: When the three young men in today's first reading refuse to compromise their religious convictions by worshiping a pagan idol and are thrown into a fiery furnace to die, they are not sure that anything miraculous will happen. But these young men tell King Nebuchadnezzar that even if God does not save them, they would rather die than betray their beliefs. This famous scene of courage in the face of violence reminds me of the central message in the 1937 book *The Cost of Discipleship*, written by German Lutheran theologian, pastor, and martyr Dietrich Bonhoeffer.

At a time when the Nazi regime was gaining power and influence in Germany, Bonhoeffer set out to explore what authentic faith looks like and to distinguish it from inauthentic or compromised faith. Bonhoeffer famously juxtaposes these in terms of "cheap grace" and "costly grace." Cheap grace is watered-down. He explains it as "grace without discipleship, grace without the cross, grace without Jesus Christ, living and incarnate." What Bonhoeffer calls "costly grace," however, acknowledges that there is indeed a cost to living the Christian life and taking the Gospel seriously.

While it may not cost us our lives, as it did for Jesus and ultimately Bonhoeffer himself, there are nevertheless consequences to standing up for our faith, especially as it relates to justice and peace in our world. There is a reason Jesus regularly warns his followers that they will have to carry their crosses and asks them if they can "drink [from] the cup" from which he drank (Matt 20:22). The three young men in the fiery furnace are models of what this "costly grace" looks like in practice.

Meditation: Lent is a time for reflecting on how we understand and live our Christian faith. What do I do when confronted with a conflict between my belief and what others might ask or expect of me? Do I only embrace a "cheap grace" when it comes to discipleship? Or do I accept the challenges of authentic discipleship in practice?

Prayer: God of all grace, you strengthen us on the journey of life and faith. Help me stay committed to your will and remain true to my Christian convictions even when I feel threatened or judged.

A Matter of Trust

Readings: Gen 17:3-9; John 8:51-59

Scripture:
"I will maintain my covenant with you and your descendants after you . . ." (Gen 17:7)

Reflection: I've often thought that at the core of human sinfulness rests a basic degree of mistrust. We don't seem to believe that God means what God says.

In today's first reading, God makes the terms of the divine covenant clear. Elsewhere in Scripture, this relationship is described simply as: "You will be my people, and I will be your God." What God relays to Abram in this passage is the divine promise to uphold the covenant indefinitely. So why do we as a human family continually ignore or dismiss God's word? To borrow from a Billy Joel lyric, perhaps "it's always been a matter of trust." We simply do not trust God; we convince ourselves that we alone are worthy of trust. This is the same dynamic that undergirds the first human sin in the Garden of Eden, playing out again and again.

God is straightforward with humanity, making it clear where the divine stands in relation to creation. God invites us into a life of joy and interdependent relationship with our fellow humans and all creation. But it isn't enough for us. Perhaps we think it is all just "too good to be true," or maybe, on some level, we just don't believe we are worthy of so great a gift from God.

Today's Gospel reminds us that Jesus is God incarnate and that his words and deeds point to the already existing covenant with God. All we have to do to participate in the reign of God is to live out that covenant. It's simply a matter of trust.

Meditation: We live in an age of individualism. We are constantly being told, in overt and subtle ways, that we must look out for ourselves first and help others only when our comfort, wealth, and safety are secured. Do I live in such a way as to reflect trust in God? How can I strengthen my faith in God's love and live more freely for God and others?

Prayer: God of truth and justice, you always call us to deeper relationship with you and one another. Give me the grace to trust you more soundly and to live in a way that reflects your love in the world.

What Is Your Foundation?

Readings: Jer 20:10-13; John 10:31-42

Scripture:
My God, my rock of refuge,
  my shield, the horn of my salvation, my stronghold!
    (Ps 18:3)

Reflection: In the Gospel of Matthew, Jesus says that those who listen to him and do the will of God are like prudent builders who construct their houses on firm foundations. Conversely, those who do not act on his words are fools who build their houses on sand, which cannot support the structure when rain, wind, and floods strike (Matt 7:24-27). When I hear today's psalm proclaimed, it is this image that immediately comes to mind. Psalm 18 celebrates the sure foundation that is God, and it challenges us to examine who or what we choose as the foundation of our lives.

For some people, the foundation of life is the quest for success or renown. This motivation governs their thinking and decision-making. For some people, the foundation of life is lust for wealth or power. They appropriate everything they can, acquiring more and more, prioritizing their own material desires over the needs of others. And for some people, the foundation of life is comfort or safety. They simply wish to be left alone, to enjoy their lives without being bothered by the struggles and difficulties of others.

But those who choose God as the foundation of their lives see the world, themselves, and God differently. They recognize their inherent interdependence, their reliance on the divine for all that is good, and the call to think beyond their own interests and concerns. Jesus models what it looks like to have God as the foundation upon which we build the structure of our lives. This way of life will not always be easy or comfortable, but, as the psalmist reminds us, God will always be our help and support.

Meditation: As Christians, we know we ought to have God as our foundation and our source of strength. But who or what is the actual foundation of my life? What do I see as the anchor and motivation for my thinking and behavior, especially as I relate to others? Where is God inviting me to lay a new foundation this Lent?

Prayer: God my rock, whether we realize it or not, you are the source of all that exists. Help me recall that you are the foundation of everything I am and the one who sustains everything I do.

No Good Deed Goes Unpunished

Readings: Ezek 37:21-28; John 11:45-56

Scripture:
So from that day on they planned to kill him. (John 11:53)

Reflection: Growing up in a culturally (and at times even stereotypically) Irish-Catholic household meant that I learned many old adages from my parents and grandparents. The most popular sayings expressed the Irish superstition that haunted our interpretation of many events. You might know some of the top hits, like "Just waiting for the other shoe to drop" or "That's Murphy's Law!" The one that best summarizes the spirit of today's Gospel is "No good deed goes unpunished," something I heard often whenever someone performed a kindness that backfired, or generosity was returned with indifference or even hostility.

Today's Gospel picks up where the miracle story of Jesus raising Lazarus from the dead left off. This excerpt is located almost at the center of the Gospel of John and marks a distinctive turning point in Jesus' ministry. Jesus had already been drawing negative attention from local authorities in response to his healing and preaching ministry, but with the raising of Lazarus, things take a more urgent and negative turn. It seems that Jesus' "good deed" will not go unpunished.

There is, of course, a notable irony in the scorn and eventual punishment Jesus receives for merely doing God's will, accomplishing surprising acts of generosity and healing, and preaching the good news of inclusion and love. So why should we as Jesus' followers expect anything different?

This hard truth of Christian discipleship is often avoided. For many of us, being a Christian is a simple and undemanding identity. But is that what Christian discipleship is all about?

Meditation: Jesus did everything right and was nothing less than the fullest expression of God's love and mercy. And yet he received scorn and punishment in response to his generosity. What do I expect that following Jesus will entail? Am I willing to face negative consequences for doing the right thing and proclaiming the gospel in word and deed? How can I more closely follow Christ?

Prayer: God of love, you call us to love as you first loved us. Jesus demonstrated this to all he encountered, regardless of the personal cost. Help me love as he loved.

April 13: Palm Sunday of the Passion of the Lord

Entrances Matter

Readings: Luke 19:28-40; Isa 50:4-7; Phil 2:6-11; Luke 22:14–23:56 or 23:1-49

Scripture:
Christ Jesus, though he was in the form of God,
did not regard equality with God something
to be grasped. (Phil 2:6)

Reflection: The scene of Jesus entering Jerusalem on a donkey as throngs of excited people shout "Hosanna!" and lay palms and coats on the road to create a royal path has been etched into our imaginations. The first of our two Gospel readings today recounts that event and encourages us to think about the beginning of Jesus' last week in terms of exaltation and glory. But, as we know, things will not go as this entrance might suggest. Many of those caught up in the celebration of Jesus' arrival will soon abandon him out of fear or confusion.

Our second reading from Paul's letter to the Philippians describes another entrance—not one of celebration and exaltation, of hope and expectation, but of God's embrace of humility and vulnerability. It is the story of God's entrance into the created world as part of that very same world, not reserving divine power and insight behind a façade of pseudo-humanity, but willfully choosing to surrender any claim to authority and divinity in order to become simply and fully human. God draws near as one of us. And the response of humanity to that perfect act of divine love? Nothing short of rejection.

This contrast between two types of entrances invites us to think about how we move through life and enter into various settings. The divine self-emptying we see in Philippians reminds us that God models a way of being that insists that the powerful, comfortable, wealthy, and privileged voluntarily surrender such grandiosity to enter into greater solidarity with the entire human family.

Meditation: God freely chooses to be emptied of the power and control that is unique to divinity in order to become vulnerable and in communion with all people. Where are the areas in my life where I am being invited to let go, to empty myself so I may enter into deeper relationship with others?

Prayer: God of humility, you entered the messiness of our broken world and experienced life as we do. Help me see myself and others as you do, and guide me on the path toward solidarity and communion.

Mixed Motives and Self-Reflection

Readings: Isa 42:1-7; John 12:1-11

Scripture:
He said this not because he cared about the poor . . .
(John 12:6)

Reflection: Amid the busyness of Holy Week each year, I never before noticed one interesting aside in the Gospel of John that we hear proclaimed today. Days before he is betrayed and executed, Jesus is at the home of some of his closest friends: Martha, Mary, and Lazarus. Many of Jesus' followers are with him, including Judas Iscariot. The Gospel passage recounts the scene of Mary anointing Jesus' feet with expensive perfumed oil and Judas responding with outrage, claiming he is upset that the oil was not sold and the proceeds used to support the poor. The Gospel narrator then tells us that Judas didn't really care about the poor, but that he was selfishly focused on how he could have benefited from an influx of money.

It's easy to pile on Judas. Although he is the proximate cause of Jesus' arrest, the truth is that Jesus' enemies were looking for an opportune time to capture him with or without Judas's help. Nevertheless, this brief aside in the Gospel about Judas's motives prompts us to reflect on our own motivations. Why do we do or say what we do? Do we say or do one thing for the sake of appearances (like Judas, claiming to care about the poor) but actually think or believe something else?

That Jesus was aware of his impending death, having talked about it with his followers for some time, suggests that there were more urgent matters calling for Judas's attention. How often do we miss important moments in life because we are focused on ourselves or worked up about some false outrage? How can we stay focused on what really matters this Holy Week?

Meditation: We live in polarizing times. It is easy to be worked up about an array of issues, and our feelings may sometimes be justified. But we may also be inclined toward outrage for mixed or even false motives. As I reflect on my own life, where do I need to be more like Mary of Bethany and less like Judas?

Prayer: God, you know me inside and out. Strengthen me to look inside and examine my motivations, guide me in speaking and acting with integrity, and direct me in following your will.

Social Media or Prophecy?

Readings: Isa 49:1-6; John 13:21-33, 36-38

Scripture:
I will make you a light to the nations,
   that my salvation may reach to the ends of the earth.
   (Isa 49:6)

Reflection: In the age of social media influencers and viral internet stars, there is a palpable tension between the allure of fame and the prophetic discipleship God expects of us. It is interesting to see how many young folks (and some not-so-young folks!) long for massive public recognition and affirmation. This desire for fame or celebrity is usually connected to a particular vision of success, one that will supposedly lead to happiness. Those who are held up as models of this sort of success—those with millions of social media followers, for example—seem to have lives that are enjoyable and luxurious, and certainly *not* difficult or painful.

In what is widely known as the second Suffering Servant Song, the prophet Isaiah proclaims to the people of Israel a very different path toward becoming "a light to the nations" than what is presented in contemporary social media. First, the reality of actual suffering is assumed. It is not easy to live according to God's hope for us, especially when it requires sacrificing individual desires, comforts, power, and wealth for the sake of the broader community. Second, the path toward becoming "a light to the nations" is shaped by God's will and not our own ambitions. Third, the reward is, as Isaiah notes, arriving at a point where we no longer rely solely on ourselves, but where "God is now [our] strength."

This way of thinking is counterintuitive in our own age. But as we continue to venture toward Calvary this week, we continue to reflect on what guides our hearts, minds, and actions.

Meditation: Our readings today are not telling us that God wants us to suffer, but that genuine relationship with God and one another requires an openness to the possibility of difficulty, rejection, and suffering. Where do I find myself resisting God's call? What can I do in these remaining days of Holy Week to better respond to God's will?

Prayer: God of love, you never abandon us nor leave us to suffer alone. Give me the courage to be a better disciple, to choose the needs of community over my own individual interests, so that I may be a true light in a world marred by darkness.

"Spy Wednesday" or Mirror of Reality?

Readings: Isa 50:4-9a; Matt 26:14-25

Scripture:
"What are you willing to give me if I hand him over to you?"
(Matt 26:15)

Reflection: I have always had something of a soft spot in my heart for Judas Iscariot. I'm not defending his actions, nor am I making Judas out to be a hero in any way. I believe that he is responsible for his actions. But I also think the way he has been vilified without nuance does not do justice to him, Jesus, or us.

It is worth remembering that Jesus saw something in Judas, up to the very end. Judas was in Jesus' inner circle, present as he traveled and invited into discussions and meals at very important moments in Jesus' life, including his last days. Some have said that Judas was merely misguided, that he simply wanted to exert pressure on Jesus to become the Messiah that Judas imagined him to be rather than the Messiah that Jesus actually was. But I don't believe that explanation helps us fully appreciate the role Judas plays for us today.

This day is sometimes referred to as "Spy Wednesday" on account of today's Gospel passage recounting Judas's agreement to betray Jesus. I have never liked that title because I believe it conveniently places all the blame on Judas like a scapegoat. Instead, today we must face the uncomfortable truth that we are not that different from Judas. Rather than fantasizing that Judas was some kind of spy or evil double agent, let's take him at face value as a genuine follower of Jesus who, while well-meaning, makes mistakes and misunderstands how to be an authentic disciple.

For Judas there is a literal betrayal, but for each of us, there are times when we compromise what we believe for the sake of our own interests. Sometimes we convince ourselves that we are doing the right thing, but in the end, hurt and betrayal are left in our wake. Perhaps we are not that different from Judas after all.

Meditation: What are some of the ways I betray Jesus? When do I put my personal interest, ambition, comfort, or security ahead of my call to Christian discipleship?

Prayer: God of mercy, you know the hearts of all people. Help me see the ways that I act like Judas, and give me the grace to turn my ear to listen always to your Son.

We Are the Body of Christ

Readings: Exod 12:1-8, 11-14; 1 Cor 11:23-26; John 13:1-15

Scripture:
"This is my body that is for you. Do this in remembrance of me." (1 Cor 11:24)

Reflection: One of the most influential sermons ever preached on the Eucharist was delivered by St. Augustine of Hippo more than sixteen hundred years ago. I think about this sermon every Holy Thursday as we commemorate the institution of the Eucharist.

In Augustine's "Sermon 272," the great Doctor of the Church unpacks the theology of the *Corpus Christi*—the Body of Christ. He begins by affirming that what appears as bread and wine to the senses of the body are recognized as the sacramental presence of Christ to the senses of faith: "My friends, these realities are called sacraments because in them one thing is seen, while another is grasped."

But Augustine does not stop there. He goes on to explain: "If you want to understand the body of Christ, listen to the Apostle Paul speaking to the faithful: 'You are the body of Christ, member for member' (1 Cor 12:27). If you, therefore, are Christ's body and members, it is your own mystery that is placed on the Lord's table! It is your own mystery that you are receiving! You are saying 'Amen' to what you are: your

response is a personal signature, affirming your faith. . . .
Therefore, be a member of Christ's body so that your 'Amen'
may ring true!"

St. Augustine recognized that in addition to the sacramental presence of Christ in bread and wine, the Body of Christ is made present in its members—you and me. When we proclaim "Amen" at Communion, it is not merely an affirmation of Christ's presence in the Eucharist, but also an affirmation of Christ's presence in the assembly of the faithful. In this way, St. Augustine reminds his hearers that we are meant to "be what we see" and "receive what we are" at every celebration of the Eucharist.

Meditation: It can be easier to say "Amen" to the eucharistic species than to the presence of Christ in our neighbors. Where do I need to be more attentive to the presence of Christ?

Prayer: God of life, you nourish us with the presence of Christ in the Eucharist and give us food for the journey of faith. Open my eyes to see Christ in those around me and to remember that we are the Body of Christ in this world.

April 18: Friday of the Passion of the Lord (Good Friday)

We Are There

Readings: Isa 52:13–53:12; Heb 4:14-16; 5:7-9; John 18:1–19:42

Scripture:
Oppressed and condemned, he was taken away,
 and who would have thought any more of his destiny?
  (Isa 53:8)

Reflection: It's common for the faithful to sing the classic African American Spiritual "Were You There?" on Good Friday. The somber, reflective, even haunting tune is familiar to many of us, and the lyrics invite us to imagine ourselves at the foot of the cross on this tremendous and terrible day: *Were you there when they crucified my Lord? Were you there when they crucified my Lord? Oh, sometimes it causes me to tremble, tremble, tremble. Were you there when they crucified my Lord?*

Living two millennia after the state execution of Jesus of Nazareth, we might find ourselves responding to this hymn's central question with an unequivocal "no." No, we weren't there when they crucified the Lord. No, we weren't there when they nailed him to the tree or when the sun refused to shine. But that is only true if we think about Good Friday in a limited, literal way.

While the murder of an innocent man who was also God incarnate is the proximate focus of today's liturgy, the injustice of what unfolded at Golgotha challenges us in our own time to think about the many ways Christ continues to be crucified. Where are we when governments continue to execute people convicted of crimes? Where are we when members of particular races, ethnicities, religions, sexualities, or genders are harassed, abused, or even killed? Where are we when all life on this planet is threatened, human climate refugees are ignored or abandoned, and various species are forced into extinction?

Christ continues to be crucified today in these and other forms of violence and injustice. This Good Friday, we might think about this hymn differently. We are in fact present at the crucifixion of the Lord in our own time.

Meditation: Do I "tremble, tremble, tremble" as much for those who are treated with injustice and violence in our time as I do for Jesus of Nazareth? How might I better see the connection between what happened to Jesus and what happens in the world today? How is God calling me to respond?

Prayer: God of the living and the dead, you never abandon those you have loved into existence. Help me see the ways your Son continues to be crucified, and strengthen me to fight against that injustice in any way I can.

Waiting in Ordinary Time

Readings: Easter Vigil: Gen 1:1–2:2 or 1:1, 26-31a; Gen 22:1-18 or 22:1-2, 9a, 10-13, 15-18; Exod 14:15–15:1; Isa 54:5-14; Isa 55:1-11; Bar 3:9-15, 32–4:4; Ezek 36:16-17a, 18-28; Rom 6:3-11; Luke 24:1-12

Scripture:
Seek the LORD while he may be found,
   call him while he is near. (Isa 55:6)

Reflection: For many of us, Holy Saturday is a weird and uncomfortable time. There is a temptation to rush too quickly from the pain of Good Friday to the celebration of Easter. Because of this, I try to focus on the first part of the day rather than quickly moving to the great Easter Vigil.

One source of inspiration that has helped me rest in the space of Holy Saturday is the great twentieth-century Jesuit theologian Karl Rahner. In his 1969 book *Grace in Freedom*, he offers a short reflection on this distinctive moment in our church year: "Holy Saturday is a strange day, mysterious and silent. It is a day without a liturgy. This is, as it were, a symbol of everyday life which is a mean between the abysmal terror of Good Friday and the exuberant joy of Easter. For ordinary life is also mostly in between the two, in the center which is also a transition and can only be this."

So how do we live in the "strange day" Rahner describes? The challenge may be finding God in the ordinariness, even when it seems difficult or God appears absent. Isaiah exhorts us in this evening's great liturgy to "Seek the LORD" and call upon God. Maybe that's what today is primarily about. It is an opportunity to practice finding God in the in-between moments of ordinary life, faithfully seeking the Lord amid the unremarkable times of everyday living. Perhaps in doing so, the mysterious and silent character of this day will become less strange, and God will become more recognizable in our daily lives.

Meditation: In a noisy and distracting age such as ours, silence and stillness can be challenging. Holy Saturday is a particularly quiet day, which invites us to discover and spend time with God. What keeps me from "seeking the Lord" in the ordinary times? Do I avoid silence, stillness, and quiet? How might I live Holy Saturday differently this year?

Prayer: God of silence, Scripture reminds us that you are not necessarily found in the exceptional events of history but in the silent whisper of ordinary life. Give me the grace to seek you where you are found and rest in the quiet of your peace.

Encountering Jesus on the Way

Readings: Acts 10:34a, 37-43; Col 3:1-4 or 1 Cor 5:6b-8; John 20:1-9 or Luke 24:1-12 or 24:13-35

Scripture:
[H]e was made known to them in the breaking of bread. (Luke 24:35)

Reflection: For the last several weeks we have journeyed together, preparing ourselves for this day of celebration through prayer, fasting, and almsgiving. We have reflected on Sacred Scripture and examined our consciences, striving to be better disciples of Jesus Christ.

Those who attended the Easter Vigil or participated in an Easter morning liturgy heard a Gospel account of the discovery of the empty tomb. But most people don't know that the church includes another Gospel story for those who celebrate an Easter liturgy in the afternoon. This story is not about the empty tomb but about what happens later when two disciples are walking away from Jerusalem and encounter a stranger along the way (Luke 24:13-35).

Known as the appearance on the road to Emmaus, this story has always struck me as a great Easter Gospel. Whereas the empty tomb narratives express an important historical moment at the heart of our faith, the Emmaus story reveals the ongoing and personal way Christ continues to draw near to us. The experience of the two disciples is relatable—they are preoccupied by the news of Jesus' execution and therefore distracted from recognizing that the Risen Christ is literally right beside them. How often are we engrossed in our daily lives, the ups and downs of our own experiences, such that we cannot see how Christ is right beside us?

What we come to learn is that our eyes are opened to the presence of Christ already in our midst through Sacred Scripture and the Eucharist. As Easter people, we are richly blessed when we gather as a community, where Christ continues to unpack God's word through the Holy Spirit and gives himself to us in the gift of the Eucharist.

Meditation: God calls us to be a resurrection people, to live every day with the joy we celebrate today. Christ is already close to us, walking alongside us, helping us see God's will and love for us. What prevents me from recognizing the presence of Christ? How can I live Easter joy every day?

Prayer: God of resurrection, the power of your love is greater than death. Open the eyes of my heart to recognize how Christ draws near as I journey through life. Strengthen my faith so I may live in Easter joy.

References

Introduction
Thomas Merton, *Seasons of Celebration: Meditations on the Cycle of Liturgical Feasts* (New York: Farrar, Straus and Giroux, 1965), 113.

Pope Francis, Apostolic Exhortation *Evangelii Gaudium*, The Joy of the Gospel (Vatican City: Libreria Editrice Vaticana, 2013), 6.

March 23: Third Sunday of Lent
Catherine Mowry LaCugna, *God for Us: The Trinity and Christian Life* (San Francisco: HarperSanFrancisco, 1993).

March 28: Friday of the Third Week of Lent
Pope Francis, Homily for the Papal Mass for the Possession of the Chair of the Bishop of Rome, Basilica of St. John Lateran, April 7, 2013.

March 30: Fourth Sunday of Lent
Pope Francis, Encyclical Letter *Laudato Si'*, On Care for Our Common Home (Vatican City: Libreria Editrice Vaticana, 2015), 5. Citing Pope John Paul II, General Audience, January 17, 2001.

April 9: Wednesday of the Fifth Week of Lent
Dietrich Bonhoeffer, *The Cost of Discipleship*, 2nd edition (New York: Macmillan, 1963), 47.